THE DICE CUP

Fiction

Flying to Nowhere
The Adventures of Speedfall
Tell It Me Again
The Burning Boys
Look Twice
The Worm and the Star
A Skin Diary
The Memoirs of Laetitia Horsepole
Flawed Angel

Poetry

Fairground Music
The Tree That Walked
Cannibals and Missionaries
Epistles to Several Persons
The Mountain in the Sea
Lies and Secrets
The Illusionists
Waiting for the Music
The Beautiful Inventions
Selected Poems 1954 to 1982
Partingtime Hall (with James Fenton)
The Grey Among the Green
The Mechanical Body
Stones and Fires
Collected Poems
Now and for a Time
Ghosts
The Space of Joy
Song & Dance
Pebble & I
Writing the Picture (with David Hurn)
Dream Hunter (with Nicola LeFanu)
New Selected Poems 1983 – 2008

Criticism

The Sonnet
W. H. Auden: A Commentary
Who is Ozymandias? And Other Puzzles in Poetry

For Children

Herod Do Your Worst
Squeaking Crust
The Spider Monkey Uncle King
The Last Bid
The Extraordinary Wool Mill and Other Stories
Come Aboard and Sail Away

As Editor

The Chatto Book of Love Poetry
The Dramatic Works of John Gay
The Oxford Book of Sonnets
W. H. Auden: Poems Selected by John Fuller
Alexander Pope: Poems Selected by John Fuller

THE DICE CUP

John Fuller

Chatto & Windus
LONDON

Published by Chatto & Windus 2014

2 4 6 8 10 9 7 5 3 1

Copyright © John Fuller 2014

John Fuller has asserted his right under the Copyright, Designs
and Patents Act 1988 to be identified as the author of this work

First published in Great Britain in 2014 by
Chatto & Windus
Random House, 20 Vauxhall Bridge Road,
London SW1V 2SA
www.randomhouse.co.uk

Addresses for companies within The Random House Group Limited can be
found at: www.randomhouse.co.uk/offices.htm

The Random House Group Limited Reg. No. 954009

A CIP catalogue record for this book
is available from the British Library

ISBN 9780701188368

The Random House Group Limited supports the Forest Stewardship Council®
(FSC®), the leading international forest-certification organisation. Our books
carrying the FSC label are printed on FSC®-certified paper. FSC is the only
forest-certification scheme supported by the leading environmental organisations,
including Greenpeace. Our paper procurement policy can be found at:
www.randomhouse.co.uk/environment

Typeset in Minion by Palimpsest Book Production Ltd, Falkirk, Stirlingshire
Printed and bound by CPI Group (UK) Ltd, Croydon CR0 4YY

Contents

THE DICE CUP

In Here

I have been in here for a long time, perfectly safe, as I've always imagined myself to be. The usual sights, sounds and scents filter through. It's hard not to take them for granted, these residual and often random impressions. They always make some sort of sense. They may not clamour for attention, but they are reassuringly there. You can try to make sense of them, build up a picture. You know it's not the whole story, but it is what there is, and that's something.

It's like a hand dealt at cards. There are implicit patterns and challenges, even if you only have the haziest idea of the rules. You know the difference between a good hand and a bad hand, but you need the will to play the hand as best you can. I do my best, but the outcome is always frustrating. I can't make much sense of it, after all.

Yes, perfectly safe, but from what, I've no idea. It's not in my nature to be adventuresome in any case. I only know that there is a reason to fear, and that's the first rule of the game, and it means that you can never win.

The Dice Cup

Of the cup itself, a sort of bone-shaker, it may at least be said that it is a perfect model of the human skull, since within its bone is a willed juggling of the few known symbols that begin to map the world. And the pictures of these symbols are their own model of our subjective foolery, for they too are made of bone. Its great subject then becomes ourselves, for in it we are the creatures of the circumstances that we go on investigating in the hope that we might control or at least predict them.

Fine chance!

To revise these circumstances to a mere skeleton of their possibility suits our macabre imagination. It's as though we might claim nothing more than the poor crook of a joint, the sad tumble of knuckle-bones, as if there were after all nothing in life grand enough to point to, either in hope or determination. In the dice cup, then, life becomes not a design but a wager; not an adventure but a game; not a cry but a smile. It claims only the limited success of our knowledge of those limitations, for naturally only what is shaken within it can be shaken out of it. And of course we ourselves will in the end be nothing but bone, and not that for always.

The French have a more hopeful view of the matter, as may be suited to their rational sentiments, for the 'cornet à dés', the cone for dice, may also be the 'cornet à dès', the trumpet of 'from', the heraldic announcement of a henceforward that is always about to happen. Like the gambler, who is forever saying: 'But I will be lucky *tomorrow*,' we play the game of imagining in our play everything that it should really be in our power to enact.

Perhaps that is enough.

Cube

In human history, this shape came late to our hands. Found in nature only as crystals in the heart of rock, and at first not much different from the rock it was bedded in, it preserved its amazing secret until we developed our slow tools for the penetration of mountains.

The idea for this came from caves: if time and wind or water could create caves, then so might we. Tools we could conceive of. Time we could steal. Caves out of caves, caves within caves, were the first dreamed luxury, perhaps occurring in dreams themselves, which struggled to uncover the layers of comfort and escape that our waking life hid from us.

The other accidents of our developed life (the smouldering lightning-stump; the roll of the fruit along the spindle of its stalk) were to bequeath iron and speed. But the crystal in the cave was the frozen fountainhead of all calculation.

This shape was hidden and guarded by three pairs of opposites, each reflecting light away from it without much complication. It became the symbol of our own seclusion. It simplified, and therefore systematised, our previously incoherent notions of up and down, forwards and backwards, left and right. In this formalised space we could now live the life of arrangement and procedure. No longer the cave-life of the vagrant formless soul, but the life of considered dimensions.

In this architecture of regulated containment, constructed of planes mimicked in any malleable materials that came to hand, we began our lives afresh. The cube bred a new civility among men. For example, it made practicable the welcome of a stranger. Counting on our fingers could never divide a quantity among three: when a couple admitted a stranger, they were left guarded and suspicious at the unfairness of an approximate sharing. Calculating with the fashioned cube, however, with its six uninterfering surfaces, became a resourceful means of generosity. And as the mystical complexity of the crystalline art developed, shape upon shape, into polyhedrons of relational understanding and fractals of soul-making, so by comparison with such divine geometry we came to despise the bestial crudity of our five-fingered hands.

But this is an old story. The hand takes its revenge in rolling the dice, compelling them to perform (like unhappy creatures in a circus) the very motions that are contrary to their nature. In their tumbling, and in our unheeding laughter; in their forced motion, and in the fierce attention of our fingers; in their struggle for repose, and in our drunken goadings; although chance seems to need the advanced technology of the perfectly flat surface, for a moment of guilty release we have restored to our lives the primitive civilities of the cave.

Dice

The hand that dared the chances cast the cubes.

It closed back into itself on the table, the knuckles and joints themselves making the sympathetic shape of a knobbly square. In that moment all hope had the free status of the possible, and the mind whispered its seductive argument:

'Throughout the evening, its array of results has been objectively established. If you had predicted correctly it would have had no effect on the outcome. And yet, and yet . . .

'Think of this: if in desperation you are wanting sixes, and sixes do indeed turn up, your superstitious prediction will have been correct. What is more, an incorrect prediction made in wilful obstinacy or despair (or perhaps with the perverse thought that fortune might defy you and produce, after all, the result you really wanted) will in this case prove to be correct. The outcome is unalterable. It was always going to be so.

'Will your incorrect predictions therefore be worth making, so long as they do not by chance predict the result you really want? Is it the case that such deviousness might be profitable? To be wrong is nothing much. Better your pride suffer than your pocket. What fatuous thoughts!'

The voice in your ear petered out, defeated by its failing logic. Your eyes were locked on to the dice, which now achieved their revelatory stillness. There were the familiar patterns of value, instantaneously calculated. The single pin-point, like a box camera. The watching eyes, like a Ned Kelly mask. The careless diagonal. The corner points smugly outlining the smaller square within. The not-quite quincunx, blueprint for orchards. The full complement, the desired twin rows, success! Whatever you thought, whatever you said, they were always going to fall that way, always going to have that value.

But you did not know.

Dunce

The wall coming from behind my left shoulder meets the wall coming from behind my right shoulder: if it didn't, I might be staring down some plastered passage to infinity. As it is, each of the walls stops dead with nowhere to go, and the line of their meeting is therefore a dual and dusty ending. It creates a private space in front of me that narrows to a dim apex, a dwindling of hope for any hangings, a tight frustration for furniture, a place of utter closure. The walls have encountered each other with all the stubbornness of traffic at a crossroads. It's a gridlock of immoveable plaster, any future entirely cancelled. It's called a corner, and I am its genius.

But in another light, this line of joined surfaces, this completely vertical finality that I find myself with much leisure to ponder, unable to think beyond it or outside it to any consequence whatever, may not after all be an ending at all. Why should it not instead be a beginning, a point from which two planes have made a conspiratorial decision to set out? Not in opposite directions, of course, nor in companionship (how fickle would either of these projects have seemed, mere featureless extension or needless duplication!) but in that exactly half-way manner of all squared determination that seems to intend two wildly disparate destinations at a significant angle from each other?

Yes, that seems a much more hopeful way of looking at things. Outwards and onwards! Although the spider has had time to spin its casually receptive web, and dust gathers at the point where the two surfaces meet a third one at my feet, it must be that this is in fact the point of departure and that all possible outcomes are already accumulating behind me. I must look to it!

The Room

When I am nothing but the shape I was, for a short time further and with no thought of it continuing, I shall have no interest in what the room offers. It will always be so. The clock's nervous advances, the reticent thirst of the orchid, the plumped cushion, these provoke an expectation of involvement. But for how long will familiar shadows move among these things?

Here is an unwashed glass, the whisky already dried to the tackiness of Scotch tape. A consulted book needs replacing on a shelf. Curtains must be drawn against the fading light. These requirements invoke my imminent presence as surely as if I were already in the act of entering, my fingers on the door handle.

For a time, then, as I say, the room may be said to reveal something of me. It contains small implications and detonations, like words in a book, though it will not last so long. It will become the sacked museum of my futurity, the rewritten history of usurpers, a sad box of lies.

Dispersals

Louisa in Lisbon, Sophie in Venice, Prue in Brazil: the unreliable trail of baggage tickets, roaming mobile servers, time-zone reminders and pencilled return dates fails to dispel a primal anxiety at this simultaneous family dispersal. It may be possible in nature for the parts of the organism to be stretched or detached to a degree that defies continuity or identity. Are there not flowers that float and return to the stem? Miles of weed with a single parent? Does not the buzzing cortex of the hive control its nerve-endings in meadows of nectar beyond a second or third village? Is not the termite tower a single organism? The swerving shoal? The migrating cloud of starlings? Nature is constellated about its differentiated centres, confident in the beautiful elasticity of its licensed freedoms. The most decisive of the dispersals is reproduction, the nurtured difference, the weight, the tug, the fall, the moving on. It is the primal adventure, this colonisation of space.

Ah, but the space is terrifying! There is far too much of it. And what is all this moving on but a tentative exploration, like children in a dark cellar with linked hands? When hands are held, all life is in that contact of the skin. Far from dispersing, the whole of matter is howling to be joined up. If we could unite the family, the race, the species, and reverse its atomisation, is this what a heaven might be?

Somewhere Else

We know where they all went. They went nowhere. But the impression left is of a collective departure, as from a party that has gone on too long. As we begin to miss them, it is easy to imagine them gathering somewhere else, with relieved comments about their lucky escape ('Well, that was dire enough, wasn't it?'; 'I thought I'd never get away'; 'I suppose if I'd arrived earlier I might have enjoyed it'; 'I *was* enjoying it rather'; 'I came away much too soon: there was nothing going on'; 'Do you think anyone's still there?').

To leave is a grand gesture, a sublime carelessness in keeping, as we now see, with the attitudes that made them noticed in the first place. After all, it was only because heads turned and names were whispered that we were so aware of them. And it was their apparent unawareness of us that first helped to distinguish them. They were the ones blessed with a freedom of choice. They obeyed no obvious rules. At the height of pleasure (the noise, the jokes, the interlocking of eyes, the filling of glasses) they were the ones who knew that they were not obliged to stay. But wasn't that knowledge in fact a terrible burden?

In the game of Murder, someone taps you on the shoulder, quite unnoticed in the crowded room. That knowledge is an irrefutable sentence. It is something that you are not allowed to share with others. It is something that you must accept, even connive at. Who is it to be? The rest of us can only speculate, as yet happily untouched. The talk is louder, faces flushed. Everyone is eager for gossip, that conspiratorial commemoration of mistakes and misfortune. We are restless for a different sort of knowledge. No one is prepared to leave.

LITTLE FABLES

1. The Thistle and the Bee

Spared to save the scythe-blade, the thistle at the granite doorstep wears a foolish grin of bravado.

'Lookie,' says he, 'at the beeline to my braw bonnet. Who'd have kenned sich juice in the dry pom-pom?'

And the bee replies: 'I chanced here after a dull acre of shaven grass. Good lord, do you think I will bother to pass by again?'

2. The Spider and the Dying Man

A dying man slept upon a spider, which had no means of protest, and in the morning, when it crawled away, it said:

'There is a weight upon the world that never seems to wake, the god of broken limbs and darkness. Who knows when he will be pleased to descend again?'

The man had only with great effort turned over in bed to reach for water, and he had nothing to say at all.

3. The Marmoset and the Elephant

A young marmoset tormented an elephant by throwing rocks at it from a small cliff. The elephant looked up in exasperation.

'Do you not know,' it said, 'that I am the Maharajah's elephant, and that all the Maharajah's elephants are well-cared-for, and have names and jewellery?'

'Of course I know that,' said the marmoset. 'Why do you think I am throwing rocks at you?'

4. The Gull and the Anchor

A gull alighted momentarily on a grassy littoral, where an anchor lay rusting. Deep flakes of oxidised iron had slipped from the anchor's bow, and the heavy links of its chain were choked together. The bright eye of the gull projected a lofty unconcern.

'Help me,' moaned the anchor. 'I am too heavy here.'

'What can I do?' asked the gull. 'I can lift my own weight, no more.'

'Sing of voyages to anyone who will listen,' replied the anchor. 'Make your following cries of wind and spume. Stir their sea-faring blood. Perhaps they will find me and grease me. Perhaps they will patch and caulk their boats.'

But the gull merely looked sideways, raised his wings and took off. He was in the habit of crying out continually in any case, and knew that no one took a bit of notice. There were no more voyages to be made.

5. The Gull and the Boat

The gull was perched on the stern of the fishing boat, looking out to sea. He mimicked in his shape everything that the boat wanted to be, the beak like a prow cocked to the horizon, the feathers sculpted in a backward sweep like shaved and clinkered boards, the wind ruffling his breast like a flag. But the boat stubbornly faced the wrong way, bobbing in the winter waves, plugged to the bed of the bay.

6. The Linksman and the Furious Members

The dismissed linksman protested the incompetence of the players.

'How can they possibly blame me if they continually miss their stroke?' he said. 'I have perfected the surface of the greens as never before, a refinement of the shaven level to a theoretical and absolute smoothness. What more can they want?'

The committee were at a loss. The greens were indeed so closely mown that no golf-ball could settle there. There was nothing to grip. The ball would land and dribble a little, but never come to rest, just like the little silvery balls in a glass box puzzle. Even on the level it would never be still for long enough to be struck. No wonder that the members were furious.

It made their lives, as they claimed, entirely pointless.

But the linksman had fulfilled the terms of his contract, and consulted his solicitor with boundless, and justified, confidence.

7. The Old Man and the Cathedral

Such a very old man, living a reduced life of utter purity and bliss! He is encountered in the precincts of the cathedral, beneath the crumbling stone, among biscuity carvings of owls and virgins, sitting with closed eyes and a contented smile. It is known that he has lived his entire life here, regulated by the bronze cathedral bells and shaded by its cloister.

When they tell him how beautiful it is, and how inspiring, and how lucky he is to be uniquely there, he has no idea what they mean.

A TERRACE IN CORSICA

1. The Orange Lily

You pass by me in some version of my season. Whatever month it may be, or whatever minute, there was always an unseen time before it, and when you leave, that privacy will return. But just for now, there I am.

You might see only leaves, bunching and splaying at shin-height, broad and stiff, like blade-paddles, so finely streaked between colours that it is texture rather than colour, which is the mysterious purple that contains a version of green. I can't see it myself, but they say that the effect is promising.

The attentions of creatures are responsible for the chains of holes across a leaf here and there. You may think that to chew symmetrically from the centre and then stop is an unlikely feat imitating the bullet, and that several such in a regular line is pure ostentation. You would be wrong. In nature are no emotions, only behaviour.

And in any case you were not here then. Nor will be when I show my orange face, which hangs luminously in flags and tissue like something half-unwrapped, or yesterday's celebration. Perhaps it is always in fact yesterday, and you should have come then. Or tomorrow.

Your eyes can do nothing to change me.

2. The Owl Proust

He sits on the telephone poles above I Costi, as if to eavesdrop on the dialogues of the night. The car will disturb him, so that he flies over us above the valley a brief way, before fluttering back, curious about the crude vision of the headlights and our apparent lack of interest in the prey momentarily transfixed by them.

A great distinction, to be a bird with a face. The ringed

sleepless eyes breed Egyptian meditations. If he had a hand, with fingers and knuckles, it would always be at his cheek as he stared down at us. It is his valley, and he is alert to its ironies.

3. Des Nèfles

Don't go on talking to me when I'm not there. I'm on a mission in the other room, resolute as a determination for Jesus or the Antarctic, though only for a particular pen or an unknown word in a fat book. To linger on the threshold, hearing only half, is neither one thing nor the other.

A nèfle can't be a medlar, surely. It wouldn't blet. It doesn't look as though it would ever get sleepy. But whatever it is, it is itself. I'll look it up.

Yes, I'll be back in a minute. So much goes by without our noticing it at all. But if you keep it, it spoils. It's not the same. It's now or never. Except for our dulcet preserves, whether of jar or pen, of medlars or muddle, that may still have something of the matter after we are dead. The words that were missed are ghosted in the words that were written; the jelly is so old that it is half-syrup. But is it likely that this sweetness will last for ever?

'Des nèfles!'

4. Noon

The terrace is blessed with stillness, an accumulating withdrawal of purpose. Beyond the black shadows of the high hedge there is a small theatrical display of sea like a glittering cloth, with one transfixed sail, its unread menu of choices. There is no casting-off today. The horizon is merely a line of satisfying completion.

The cricket is motionless on the wall. There is nowhere it would rather be. The glasses and the bottle are trading their inches of air and liquid. The lily flames in the sun, content in this moment between unfolding and falling.

Nothing stirs but the imperceptible, the black figs that will split and ooze in an afternoon, the roughness of a cheek in slumber, protected by a fallen wrist and already thinking itself an old salt's beard.

5. Le Barbu, 12% vol

Rigid in the afternoon the furled sails of the pleasure yachts, intent on pleasure. The sun turns parasols into tambours. And the bearded man has doffed his cap to me, as it should be, murmuring in liquid syllables of the marvels awaiting me in sleep. His promise is absolute: my bed shall be my own still voyage, rocked in his care.

Another inch is a generosity he can easily afford. The angle of his pipe and his cheerful silhouette proclaim it. For him, nothing is lost but returns in dreams. Old salt, old label, my familiar, my garrulous prophet, my discovered brother!

6. Vieux Fromage avec les Habitants

Born in cheese, your body all cheese! Harbouring intuitions of cheese, being a Wordsworth of cheese, abandoned to sympathetic nature! Being between shapes, neither hoping nor remembering! Squeezed like a delicious blackhead, lithe and wriggling, in ignorant companionship through your planet's thick atmosphere, a disc of creamy collapse! Sleeplessness, joy, the translated stink of herds!

7. The Cricket on the Table

A premonition of wind brought the cricket to our table where a game was in progress. The mind, already scrambling and unscrambling, brought it into play. Kric, kric, kric, etc! In a trice it was on the board, stirring tiles with leisurely kicks of its neatly lifted but occasionally dragging legs. Ticker-ticker! The existing words were in danger of being reduced to indiscriminate alphabet, the tiles clicking against each other like buttering a pan. But nothing is inevitably its name. In the flickering light of the candles, their hot liquid sockets pasted with tiny moths, the cricket was nude and glistening. Its leg-joints, carried like stilts above its inching body, were pale and raw-looking, clenched with the power to propel it at any moment to the far corner of the terrace. Did it bask in the dangerous glow of the wax? It had no notion of being identified, nor could be expected to nudge together, like ouija, the approximate tiles of its name in any of the languages in which it was known. It was not a player. It was not a contender. It was a Quixote in the crusade against the Abecedarian Heresy, the cheek-plates of its gothic visor clamped in severity, plumes wavering. Let the tower of language fall! Let the fires burn! For the wind is indeed rising, and it is the hour of all dispersals.

BATTLEFIELDS

1. Power

He had deliberately put on a countenance of impassivity, with fixed eyes and flexed jaw, like a man whose loose premolar has clicked out of position and must be gently coaxed back with the tongue. If observed, he could pretend to be remembering pi beyond forty decimal places. An infinitesimal widening of the cheeks would give the impression of something like a rueful smile at the frank assessment of past errors contemplated, or future chances assessed. It was no doubt intended to be masterful, this rapt mask. Protective, above all, but communicating authority, and intelligence. No one would dare approach him and ask what he was thinking. No one would ask him if he wanted something to drink. It would be an interruption, an irreverence. This man was in the middle of a serious communion with himself.

But what *was* going on in his head? Did it matter? Was there something happening that he was neglecting to take notice of? Could anything out there be sufficiently important? No, surely not.

It would be enough to wait for him to speak. We should have a better idea then.

2. The Cannibal Pope

Rational Europe may mock or ignore in its fashion, under the benign dictatorship of the press. America's twenty thousand churches go on dancing and singing. China simply never heard of it. But how sweet this healing vote, the iron hand upon the weakening schisms, the remembrance of the blood-lore at the core of our faith! Everything that was in danger of dissipation in gift shop art, rigid rule and conference explanation, or marooned in museum relics, is now restored by the full authority of Christian Africa. How welcome the Cardinals' smoke, their grave trust in the one candidate who embodies the sublime ambiguities of the modern experience! His tribal innocence, knowing nothing but the slit nose and the kidney sizzling in the billy can, is the only quality that can now paradoxically save the whole world. From devouring to forgiveness, from enemy to friend, from marauding militia to campfire sacrament, is the tremendous gulf that only unusual devotion can bridge. His obscure career has brought a bright and fugitive fervour to a dull clerisy who had almost forgotten the humble origins and primal sacrifice of our Saviour. We flock now in our millions to the chrysoprase balcony where we kneel to his raised fingers, the incense, his grinning benison.

3. The Emperor

When I first realised that Napoleon was still alive, I was not as terrified as you might think.

To encounter that severe forehead, that decisive nose, that shrouded hand, the whole body (through which the blood still effectively pumped) perhaps concentrated over an old campaign map or relaxed, as at Wagram, with folded arms and one leg on a small table, would be a wonder. Even more so to observe a flicker of amusement in the eye, a little downturn of the mouth, as if in recollection of someone's celebrated *bêtise*.

Those who had seen it for themselves reported a flood of joy succeeded by a pathos so palpable that it was like the bouquet of an ancient wine, almost stifling in the brief moment of its passing. For the Emperor was revealed, like the statue of Hermione, as an admonitory *tableau vivant* surrounded by those who had both idolised and betrayed him: worn troupers of the Hundred Days, Bourbon opportunists, defeated generals, Bonaparte relatives who had dropped off like parasites engorged with patronage.

These were actors, of course, hired for the occasion, but at their centre was this little uniformed figure who at length turned his head to the audience and slowly opened his mouth. His lips were dry, his skin green with arsenic, the strands of hair clammy across his brow. His manner was uncertain, as if he did not quite know what to say on this momentous occasion, or if indeed he had time enough left to say it. The trappings of his dress were tawdry semblances of the embroidered coronation robes of 1804 designed by the painter David.

What was it that he said? Was it some comment relating our Europe to the Europe of his dreams? For some reason I was never told, and perhaps it was just as well. To outlive history, particularly as its decisive agent, is to become merely the shadow of a shadow.

But what was expected of him, and why was I so vaguely hopeful of a revelation? I wanted to take him to see his worn triumphal statue surrounded by four stone lions in the palm-lined square of his birthplace and tell him that although this was not the greatest of his memorials, the lions spewed the purest water day and night into the basin of the fountain, even in severe drought. I wanted to take him to his family house among the restaurants and gift shops of the old town. Above all, I would have liked a solution to the mystery of death, and to have been able to restore him to his mother and to see on her face the smile that appears on the face of all mothers when they look at their sons: benign, amused, hypnotised, the smile of rapt and exclusive attention.

The newspapers claimed that it was a trick, achievable with ease in our era of willing credulity and animatronics. DNA testing was proposed. But there was a counter-argument, by which I understood that the savants whom Napoleon had introduced into Egypt were supposed to have uncovered the most exclusive secrets of embalming, a process that had in truth at last moved beyond vain appearance into the reality of that deathless afterlife sought by the Pharaohs. Was it possible? Perhaps, then, the marble images and the fountains were unnecessary, and would now be dust long before the flesh they commemorated? I thought of that great Egyptian poem about Napoleon, Percy Shelley's 'Ozymandias', and how it took for granted the futility of empires, the desert gradually enveloping the broken statue. The poem lives. Why not the man?

But where would they take Napoleon now? And what on earth would they do with him? And what, after all, did his life amount to without his mother?

4. Impasse

If I could leave the barn, I'd be away like a stallion from a fire. The village is only a mile away, but it might just as well be on the moon. I know the way: down two fields to the drinking fountain by the sharp bend in the road, and then a good sprint in the direction of the sunset.

The sun is always sinking behind our village, shelves of red cloud like a pharmacy, and rooks rowing along in silhouette. There will be poppies by the roadside, quaking grasses, wild fennel, and tormentil, tempting you to stop and finger a bunch for the first pretty girl you meet. You think that you're never going to get home for the pouting blooms, the whiff of the hedges, with the nearby sound of grazing cows, the wet wrench of the grass-clumps and the working mouth that sounds like love-making. They were our complete freedom, those truant afternoons.

But how can we escape? We are surrounded by grenadiers who won't go until they have starved us out. I would make a dash for it, but I can only think of the way that musket-balls lodge in the flesh. They sit there as comfortably as if they had grown there, knotted in tight as cherry stones, and when the surgeon digs in, exasperated, you hear the screams long after they have stopped.

Grenadiers, just beyond the barn door, through a crack of which the sunlight floods in shafts of dust!

An infinity of golden dust, the motes of forgotten harvests visible in the dangerous light that stripes our darkness!

If they came in to get us, it would soon be over, but of course they believe that we have muskets too. The bars of light, with dust barely moving in the still air, are arrows pointing in both directions at once.

5. Confrontation

The boundary is a lolloping stream, hidden by ferns. A fence can't be posted in a stream. It must sit on one side or another.

What sleeplessness over those riparian metres! Thin and noisy as the stream is, there are eels the size of fountain pens, nudging like worrying thoughts. And a mad contortionist otter. Who wouldn't want to claim to be their fastidious guardian? Or perhaps eagerly to abandon their care? You must decide which. Is it you, old enemy, or is it I, nose to nose and glaring eyes, the private terror-grin in the mirror?

Though boundaries shift, there is no relinquishing of that precious property, the waters of life and its populations.

6. Marshal Zukhov

The gesture that the sculptor gave him was the ambiguous one of the right hand slightly raised above his horse's neck, the palm tilted back from the wrist. It was either warning or pacifying. It said either 'No further' or 'For the moment be still,' depending on who was addressed, the advancing German army or his patient horse, portrayed at a slowing trot. It is a convention of the triumphal equestrian monument that a leader be shown as having something to lead, and his horse may represent his people as much as anything. To say to them so quietly, almost with the motion of the Buddha dispelling fear, that they have power enough to bide their time, to stand sentry at the inviolate gates of Moscow, to watch their enemy retreat, is to trust to the mandate given and the absolute power assumed.

And for us, looking up at this bronze recreation of a defiant moment, it is an adequate warning. We know what it is like to have marched through the snows suffering every hardship and deprivation, our line thinning with attenuated ordnance, the motive forgotten, the object less and less likely to succeed. In our frozen delirium we may even have forgotten who we are. Are we the vain conquerors, truly? Or are we perhaps the equally deprived citizenry, shivering in our assailed redoubt? Perhaps in the end it does not matter, and the Marshal is merely our version of the Archangel who forbids any return to the garden where men may have once supposed themselves entitled to be happy.

It was only recently, therefore, and in wonder, that I saw the Marshal brought on his bier through the half-lit rooms of a wine cellar. He was one of a succession of bodies carried on simple trestles that perhaps designated them as traitors, or men defeated by political fashion. As he passed me, the

Marshal's mouth (and indeed the whole of his head) was flipped open for me, two circles side by side like the hinged lid of a Kilner jar, as if to demonstrate the irrevocable shame. Though the mouth seemed to be entirely filled with metal teeth, some of them centrally placed and interlocking with the others by a mechanism of cogs with deep workings, like an old watch, beneath them was surely a tongue still glistening. And when the mouth was opened, had there not come to me a deep sigh, as if in weary hope of release?

'Stop!' I exclaimed. 'He's still alive!'

But they closed the head again, and went on their way. All his great services to his country! His place in history! Was this torture performed at someone's vile and thoughtless whim? I knew it was not my place to make a scene.

7. The Remnant

i. Pelorus

When the fighting stopped, I was out on my feet, staring downwards, the heel of my left palm cupped to the knee, sword sweated to my right with a senseless clutch, the blade trembling against the soil like the cane of a blind man. The air was thick as water; it re-entered my lungs in roars of applause. When I looked round, I could see that there were only five of us left, the others sunk to their hams or crawling over the bloodied flints with looks of disbelief. We had been spared.

ii. Hyperenor

I remember that we came out of the ground in pain, like an aching jaw, waking to the din of metal and indiscriminate attack. Now we are a significant remnant, heroic handful, combat corps. There is dragon in our blood, and when we ejaculate it feels like the grinding of teeth. We will descend into Thebes, take wives and remember the dragon. To survive armies is to live for ever.

III. *Chthonius*

We were unique, inseparable like the fingers of a hand, working together to get a grip on the situation, back to back, fighting off what seemed to be a deadly future. But one by one we outlasted our fate. Nycteans brings me orchids, which remind me of warriors, packed with grey pouches, strugglers living on air. They brandish their white shields veined with blood.

IV. *Udaeus*

Now we are granted visions. In my dreams I can wriggle and push towards the light in my bee helmet. One jump and the splayed legs drift, boots filled with water, in a swarm of tiny snails. I will punch my way back into the air, or so I think, but the flooded fields are a living ceiling of grasses and my breath escaping is a trickle of bubbles on the quiet stems of pale and sunless fronds. After a while I don't know whether I am now growing here, burrowing my way in,—or breaking free, a tadpole with alarming hieroglyphs of legs. I wake to a world of prophecy: my daughter will give birth to Tiresias, who will listen for a time to my old-soldierly babble and then go on to greater things.

34

v. *Echion*

The remnant became an elite and flowered as kings. Not the
last, but the first. Not ten boots in a field, but five grey heads.
I am father to Pentheus, King of Thebes; Chthonius is
grandfather to Polydorus, King of Thebes. The kings will
beget kings, and the law will breed laws. All wars have legends
like these.

I may remember the fighting, but I will know the law. I
may remember the frieze of five sown men and the chance
of their spared lives, but I will know the law. I may still die
in blood, but I will know the law.

Not a remnant, but a dynasty.

THE OTHER WORLD

1. Low Tide

At low tide, the relics. Old jetty stumps and sunken wheels for boats. Gritty clay reefs, the memory of infant thumbs and frowns. Unaccustomed stretches of sand with pained expressions and bristling worm-holes like Keats's life mask, half-smiling through a straw.

What do we say below the line of weed?

'Give me your hand, old pace-maker. I have your heart already.'

Arm-in-arm and out-of-step, like the three-legged race, with occasional splashes. We are skirting our mysterious origins and our words are wilful marginal glosses on an eternal text. This is in fact, though its best-known, its least characteristic appearance, all surface, with the skin lightly drawn back by the perigee.

2. The Pool

In the rocky pool the semicircular wall of stones is like an arm protecting school work from the curious gaze of a neighbour. It is neither high enough nor complete enough to prevent the sea from investigating, but that was never its intention. It was constructed idly, in a long moment of unconcern. It was a gesture of playful privacy, with nothing to hide. Small boulders balanced on others hardly bigger, pebbles stowed in the crevices, shingle dribbled over. The wall did not even reach the surface of the lapping water, which showed little interest in it, shrugging a little, moistening the stones, then retreating.

Now the air is loud with impatience, and the sea hurtles over itself in its eagerness to reach the shore. The weight of water sweeping in, swirling and retreating, dislodges the stones and slowly the frail fragment of wall rejoins the shifting floor of the foaming pool. The sea has found nothing and understands nothing, and rages in ignorance like any bully.

3. Snails

At three o'clock, the sea in the pebbly shallows has warmed to the still-tolerable temperature of the third breakfast coffee. The sunlight, even in the further depths, moves in interconnected patterns of elastic skeins and rhomboids that contract and expand above the stones and boulders, illuminating the fine vegetation that clings to them like down on surfaces of skin. The light is a tender caress as if from another world that has only imagined them.

It is at this time of day that the snails emerge, drawn by the afternoon warmth to bask on the stones. Each stone possesses its tiny snail, like a coiled castle on an eminence, with only one entrance to the spiral summit. Or like the nipple of a breast, insentient but expectant, urged by the sunlight to a solitary indulgence in exposure. Perhaps they are grazing now, these creatures, driven to feed, and careless of danger. Each on its stone, each the still point of the ever-moving reticulation of sunlight.

4. The Shoal

I have grown fins that propel me over the sea bed, on which the sunlight shifts like a screen of static about to resolve itself into a picture. I pass the sprawl of pebbles four feet down, the fallen slabs, the deep pool, the shoulders of smooth rock, the clumps of weed, the cooler depths at twenty feet, bluer, darker. The fish swim with me, and I am one of them, an oblade, the eleventh of eleven, swimming in the wake of their penny shoal. The shimmying of their tails, the sudden change of direction, the nervous darting, all suggest that they are aware of me. But at the same time there is a determination to be somewhere else in due course, a sense of destination. Nothing could deter me from following. Nothing could be more threatening than I am myself, but look! They have accepted me, and no other predator would be ready to take me on. I am the lookout, riding post. I am their herdsman, their protector. The sea has no boundaries.

5. The Shoal: a palinode

Soon enough I find myself alone, unaware of any divergence. It feels like a trick that time has played. Where have they gone? How do I know where I am going?

I turn, and find a pair of eyes behind me. And another. And another. Glazed in an expression of unconcern. They even half turn away, in a show of stubbornness. Are they now following me? Turning contains stasis. I have turned. They have turned. It is a moment when nothing at all might happen.

And as always, in continuous movement, incurious about any of us, follower or followed, the green glimmers below, the silver swirls above.

6. Amphibious

We are so often half in and half out of this other world of ours that its strangeness becomes almost commonplace, and yet whatever it gains by way of familiarity never fails by the end to strike us as quite odd. It is simply, you might say, that we don't belong here. We judge the quality of our experience not by opinion, but in the light of received memories of previous occasions, which we have longed for or disbelieved. These seem quite unrelated to life as it is really lived.

But why does this world so intrigue us?

'I could get used to this,' I cried. 'And if I were more accustomed to it, it might at last seem truly appropriate to my skills and needs.'

But there was no question of improving the experience, finding it useful for anything, or being able to pass on advice. To those who are already tourists of their own lives there is no future in collecting together the random thoughts that idly occur to you at such moments. You would be laughed at. What is really required is the discipline of a regimen, an understanding bred of the devotion of a lifetime, the unique insight of a vocation.

But still I am haunted by the feeling that it is here that I am truly alive, that everything exists for this mesmeric forgetfulness, this translation and ecstatic change of gravity.

7. The Deep

You can always go deeper into your fear, deeper than you really care to go. Look at the silent herds below you on the slopes of the ocean's mountains, pulsing and luminous! They show bright knobs and stalks, winking antennae, jaws like basins of teeth, whole bodies turned inside out. You have no kinship with these sports of nature, but must consider them carefully for the traits that might betray qualified ambition or rational anxiety. No? None of these?

At any rate they are in no position to enter your world, sly and rivalrous, or exponentially multiplying. Exhale and rise, with a trail of bubbles! Leave that cold carnival, wake to the warm and human air!

LIMBOS

1. The Village Sage

There is always a need to pass through the dolls and windmills to reach the fruit rotting on the branches. I packed just too many books: I could leave one carelessly in the café to impress the girl who flapped the wings of an indigo eagle printed above her coccyx every time she returned to the zinc counter. Like a votive constellation, its body was a mere plotting of pinpricks, and it floated in the minds of the idle customers. Here is the village sage.

'Monsieur,' I said. 'I can see that you are a man after my own heart. You can sit here, day after day, barely noticing the fresh headlines on the news-stands or the water cart slaking the dust at your feet. You have better things to think about.'

His two eyes were trembling pools of disquiet, held with precarious self-control on the brink of spillage. His mouth opened slightly, as though with the memory of an habitual disputatiousness, but he did not speak.

Was this choked emotion the result of a long-reasoned metaphysical enquiry? Or was it the simple projection of a personal despair? To be the acknowledged sage even of a blind-shuttered village straggling the highway is a great state of affairs, but there is not much daily satisfaction in it.

I could move on from here, or I could stay. As perhaps he once had.

2. The Hourglass

He writes this in his dream book, taking stock, turning the glass on its head for what it will teach him of how long it all might take. No time at all, she whispers, while her eyes blow up like howitzers, making horizons. So it began. Well, it's already started. It's running through as steadily as a film, grainy as natural light caught unawares. Above, the stillness collapsing, the bulk shouldering its silo, all its chances undermined. Below, gravity only, and small spilth.

Counting the sand grains told him something, stroking each hand's careful forefingernail against the tablecloth and always one left over, one grain unmatched. So time, which is always what you have and always also what you have already had, the unknown and the known, is never fairly balanced in the glass, never a moment of strange equipoise, some narrow absence linking its enlargements.

It's over, then, before you barely know it, a last dry dribble, defining empty space, a portrait of sand as useless rearrangement.

Just as the full eggcup mirrors the hourglass and any such breakfast must become a hat, so her lowered eyelid is an empty shell. Did he imagine that she herself took up that windowed dumb-bell? Did she turn it over? The dream book hasn't much to say about it.

Shadows on the wall, and little more. A miniature intense light, spooling for ever and ever, waiting for eyes to be born. Waiting for something decisive to occur, the ring of fire to be broken.

He moves the waisted glass away from him, not in rejection (as if to say, the time's used up and never to be used again), nor in a vain desire to save that time (as if to say, fill up my glass again!), but as a challenge, equally risk and threat, a defiant gesture, a determination not to succumb, like lifting and settling a bishop squat down some short half-blocked diagonal.

His turn will come again. The rules say so. And after all, little has happened yet. Can time itself run out, as in a game?

It makes an almost silent sighing sound, a tiny curtain

drawn round Titania sleeping, the limp of the sandman tapping at her shell. And he invades her palindrome of dreams, pulls the hours backward like a wind against him, moving in silence like a grandmother. And yet he cannot move. There is a crawling desert at his feet. It mounts the ankles. Nothing is in his head. The skull is cracked.

He has come so far, only to find her face averted. He has come so far, and yet it hasn't taken any time at all. No time at all, yet all the time there is. Moving in space to face what was already there. Nowhere at all, yet everywhere. And will she turn now? With what kind of smile? He knows it is no dreaming. He is awake. It is no sand-clock game. It is his life.

3. Suffering

Deeply honoured, we are invited after the conference into the Director's office. But do we not also confer honour, tweed weighting the coat-stand, our brief greetings defining the gravamen of continuing discussions?

'Gentlemen, we are no rabble of poets: we could be taken for doctors, academicians, statesmen!'

Is my urbanity taken for foolish ingratiation? Where is *my* hand-tailored waistcoat? Where is *my* gold watch-chain?

Above the Director's polished desk are framed the life-sized examples in mahogany, as of a temporal sequence, of his medical specialism: the stubborn survival of a man who is also a fungus. These engravings are in relief, and on closer inspection are also alive, so that I am in an instant transfixed in pity and revulsion by the suffering of something that is barely human, the textbook evidence of an extreme case of its kind, but also possessed of a fragile dignity.

The patient may be thought to be lying against a tree, as though a convention of the time placed him there in pastoral repose, the tilt of the cavalier hat suggested by the gills of a mushroom that also contains the papery elements of a face, with Dumas moustaches. How precarious an existence! How impossible such vegetable neurology! What pathos inherent in the traces of hope and swagger in the flaking recumbent figure, the inert nobility in pain, the tender flayed edifice, hardly daring to move! The penis is a knotted root, distended and detached. Nothing will come of this man. He has no idea of liberating himself. He must be kept in ignorance of his condition.

The Director emerges, drying his hands. Might he, if asked, explain to me whether his specimens, quietly stirring and imperceptibly moaning, are freaks of nature or somehow the result of a hideous cross-breeding? How can I possibly ask?

4. Outposts

The rocks lie between land and sea, belonging to neither of them and showing nothing of their established character. Land is a solid citizen, putting out its fringe of cliff-grass over nostrils and gullies where rabbits push and tumble. It wears the sea at its throat like lazy lace down there. Sea is terrified, creeping up to touch the land in disbelief and scurrying away again because the land is far taller than it seemed from the horizon.

Look at it another way. Sea becomes the leveller, making inroads with a killer's infinite patience, while land slithers and collapses. The hands on the neck of the countess, who laughs as her pearls spill. Who would suspect the murderer to appear in the drawing-room, making such a public display?

Only the slightest tightening of the playful fingers suggests the motive, and the power.

But the rocks. Ah, the rocks! They have no destiny of their own. The sea passes over them regularly, in casual possession. They are no longer land, no longer desirable. Land creatures have abandoned them, and the creatures of the sea wait, in uncertain tenancy, for the salt replenishments.

Only birds, alighting occasionally after the longest journeys, lend them a dignity that they may once have had. They become pinnacles for vigilance and for the drying of feathers. They become streaked with guano, faint green in the dirty white, as though marked for some purpose. They are outposts of a kind, though life itself, as always, goes on elsewhere.

5. *Seigneur-terrasse*

He came every day, perfectly dressed in black, with a chapeau melon, to this busy café named for an emperor, perfectly positioned at the corner of the town's main street and the square that was also named for an emperor. It seemed like a hinge of possible events, either the turning from a thoroughfare into a place of gathering (a kind of withdrawal) or the emergence from contemplation into the route that led out of town (a kind of exploit). Between the two a writer could be pleasingly caught, as though pinned at a minor crisis of his career.

He always ordered one of their tiny coffees, and sat with it like a bear at a dolls' tea party. The brown sugar, like quarried marble, was placed to one side. His hat was there, and his gloves. The cup was so small that a lump of sugar lowered into it brought the fragrant liquid almost to the brim.

Occasionally he would write something in his notebook,

and his waiter would feel proud of him: this table was *his* table, and it was the one invariably chosen by this distinguished customer, who found much to observe there.

The other waiters laughed at him. 'You are losing tips all morning. This *seigneur-terrasse* sits there for ever in front of his one coffee. He never re-orders. He never leaves. We get five or six customers apiece in the time that he is there. You think he is a distinguished person? We think he has nowhere else to go!'

But the waiter was loyal, hovering in case something further was required, but never intruding. In old age, there was only one other thing that he remembered about this customer, something that always remained a puzzle. He remembered the day when an old-fashioned carriage passed in front of the café and paused, a young lady looking out from beneath her parasol. The *seigneur-terrasse*, who had lingered on this occasion into taking lunch, rose as if from a dream and stumbled through the other tables towards her. She for her part seemed amused, as if in possession of a secret that he would dearly like to know. She raised her head to look down at him with detachment. Her lips pursed briefly in judicious appraisal. He stared up, trailing his napkin to the pavement.

One word came from him, in apparent disbelief, as if over a distance greater than that between the terrace and the enamelled carriage door. The waiter was sure that his customer exclaimed: 'Mother!' But how could this young lady be his mother? He was a middle-aged, if not elderly man, distinctly older than she was.

There was no explanation to this story. The young lady's knowing amusement seemed about to twinkle into sheer glee, while the discomfiture of the *seigneur* was absolute. Whether some chastisement or confession ensued, the waiter could not remember. He may have been distracted by another customer or some necessary duty. Even something as trivial as an uncollected tip lying like a bookmark openly and at risk on a vacated table could easily have distracted him.

He was eventually tracked down by the writer's most diligent young biographer, but even then could not be prompted to further details. In his turn, the biographer didn't think to explain to a mere waiter the reason for his quest, or what it was about his subject's anguished career that had come to a head in that café, in that town, at that particular epoch. The two smiled vaguely at each other across the recognisably unbridgeable gulf of time.

6. The Fire Log

The texture of the fire log was unnoticed until it was well alight. Cut from a square weathered post, it sat well in its deep parallel grain, worn and dried to a ridged texture, solid in its rectilinear weave. Too late to say a pity to burn it! It was unrescuable from the stove's hunger, already deeply glowing. The heat thrilled and faded like a pulse as the air was drawn across it, and the smoke drifted as it had drifted over the distant battlefields of Wellesley's Spain, obscuring the tight ranks and then revealing them, still resolute though already breaking under fire. I was myself among them, calling to companions: 'Don't despair! It isn't too late! Something can be salvaged from all this!'

But the roar of the fire was the roar of an unappeasable wind, and the grain of the wood trapped us like the deep corrugations of a ploughed field. We could not advance, and we could not run away.

7. The Porch Philosopher

Oh, have you ever heard of the world of unbroken things? Don't think I come with news of a discovery, as though original perfection were truly possible, an actuality to be found somewhere in our restless and frustrated search for it. As though the complete set, the ever-functioning machine, the lasting organ, the unfissured rock, the unfallen seed, the untrodden twig, the perfect shape, the idea itself, could indeed exist. After all, everything that we have seen we have touched. Everything that we have touched is already far removed from its conception of itself.

In any case, we are only happy in our incompleteness. The unplaceable pieces of indiscriminate sky or sea, like little sandwiches with handles; the unread chapters, containing revelations; the rock unvisited; the blank pages inviting adventures not yet dreamed, thoughts uncontemplated; the fish gaping for the hook; the cheek unkissed. Were we to find this world of unbroken things, its permanent and unapproachable self-containment would chill us to the bone.

Is God the name we give to our obsession with completion, even though we know in our hearts that such a process is illusory or unending? If so, God mocks our idea of him, twisting out of our grasp like a thief pursued. He is change, disruption and failure. We must be content to forget the world of unbroken things as an unprofitable illusion. Remember, I mentioned it only to make this commonplace point.

THE GREAT DETECTIVE

1. Evidence

The great detective effortlessly assembled all the evidence: the marble squares beneath the feet, like a game with sweetmeats, pistachio veined with rose, ochre veined with umber; receding patterns of black and grey, advancing patterns of grey and white; herons trussing a fox; friezes of leaves. Below, stairs leading to no escape; above, the cupolas of gold, the ironwork lamp-fittings, the unclimbable pillars. He noted all the surviving objects belonging to mysterious events, the glass boxes contriving at once to display and conceal the wilder implications of what they might be presumed to contain. In particular, he noted the withered foot of St Agnes of Sienna, the toes held parted as if to slip on a thonged sandal. Where was she now?

If he had not been insensitively interrupted in his lengthy enumeration of the evidence, we might easily have taken it upon ourselves to sketch our own solution. The exhaustive detail is so evocative of the missing picture that we think we are on the verge of understanding everything. But of course we are mistaken. We have been too hasty!

'Please forgive us,' we say. 'Carry on. Don't mind us. Really we have no idea at all. It was so thoughtless of us.'

How can we imagine that the great detective will not take umbrage at this? He has indeed assembled all the evidence, but is still in the torment of his reasoning.

When in possession of all the evidence, we have to understand, it will be difficult, perhaps quite impossible, to know even what the crime was.

2. The Armed Hatband

The explosions were almost hard to hear, intermittent percussive sounds with the colourful effect of the feathers of tiny birds tucked into leather. Passers-by looked round to see where they might be coming from, but saw nothing. Except, possibly, the wearer of a broad-brimmed hat turning into a doorway with a secret smile.

Who could be threatened by such squibs? They were so small as to sound distant, like Chinese festivities two streets away. But it was soon noticed that pedestrians were stopping suddenly and clapping a hand to their cheek or back of the neck, as though stung by insects.

What did it matter? And where did the perpetrator go?

After every unexplained event a mystery remains, and it not unnaturally occupies the idle hours of the great detective, toying in a café with a torn, empty tube of sugar. We believe, he suggests, in the absolute significance of trifles. They are like games that we might play ourselves. And perhaps even win.

What links the victims? What is the meaning of the choice of weapon? Is there any discernable motive? Before his coffee cools, the great detective has sketched out a solution, which conforms to his perverse theory that the magnitude of a crime lies in inverse relation to its means and purpose. It becomes a terrible weakness that links us all.

3. The Great Detective Speaks

The great detective, tired of being brought out of his frequent retirements to solve dramatic puzzles while scribbling silently on the back of a restaurant bill, leaves the city for the islands.

The passengers crowd to the rails when someone proposes that distant seals are lovely sirens in animal shape. 'But it is not for this that I have saved my life,' is the thought that occurs to each of them as the single bed-sheet is turned back.

Clothes thrown over a chair begin to rebel. Fashions have changed. The moth has been busy. They are bored with each other's company. What is there not to complain about? Will even the grand dinner prove a disappointment?

Over madeira, the captain turns to the detective:

'You, my friend. You have the answer perhaps?'

The passengers are expectant. A hand pauses in peeling a peach. They feel that they deserve miracles, or a little excitement.

4. Locked Room

He has no need of suspects, since all are considered guilty. And there is no particular victim, since all, too, are their own victims. The crime is the seed in the brain that flowers when it wants to. It is the only crime for which an alibi is useless.

From years of judging intentions by appearances he offers remarkable guesses at truth. Under his cool gaze words are unmasked as thoughts and suppressed feelings ooze beneath the stanching handkerchief of deduction.

All that he has noticed is gradually opened like a shape from marble, for the facts are always there for us. We should not otherwise be able to recognise his discoveries at all, nor delight in our ignorance. Now we are better able to follow him, just a step behind, when he discloses all that he has saved for the final chapter. Only the smashing of the geode will reveal its treasures.

5. Diagnosis

Naming is a fear, since nothing can be known until named. As the eye moves across shapes in a room without really seeing anything it has no words for, so the mind is happily ignorant of all that might destroy it.

Which is why we are so willing to enter those dark diverging paths of the wonderful wood of forgetting. We're ready to lose everything by not knowing that we once possessed it. We yield it up to oblivion, like a votive incense, like an appeasement. We create our own problems.

But naming is our compulsion. It is the instrument of our knowledge and the gift that is our undoing. So diagnosis becomes a self-fulfilling prophecy, the fatal future that we have unknowingly arranged. And who better to provide the answers for us, to astound us, to remind us of what we should have known, ultimately to defeat us, than the great detective? We are drawn to him, and our consultation is our undoing.

6. Wanted

There were new posters everywhere, framing haunted faces, handbills with easily-recognised personalities, the small fame of the streets. Were these posters mourning the sufferers of crime or warning of its perpetrators? Around every corner the same badly-printed hollow eyes stared out, like those of beggars, appealing defiantly to the public.

Passers-by looked away and pretended to notice almost anything else instead: windows full of millstone cheese or dusty dolls, well-dressed dogs leading old ladies, blown newspaper. They preferred the least of the life they recognised.

This might be a problem for the great detective. But the cases he is vowed to investigate must be unique. Here was simply another general example of the confusion between criminal and victim, proving how ridiculously easy it is to disappear, as both criminals and victims do. As we all do.

7. The Greatest Crime

In his prime, conducting his most celebrated cases, he was universally admired. He undertook the impossible and teased the police. He predicted the discovery of clues and compelled confessions. His systematic deductions were analysed in faculties of philosophy and women attached themselves to him outside courtrooms in throes of fluttering devotion.

'La, la! The great detective!'

But for him, however bizarre the crime or complex the mind of the criminal, the triumphs of successful deduction were not enough. It dawned on him that the greatest crime of all, the most outrageous defiance of the profoundest law, is not only insoluble but occurs so frequently that it is not seen to be a crime at all. And no wonder, for this crime, while it clearly has a victim, can't be said to have a perpetrator. And indeed, its universal occurrence is its justification, for without penalty of any kind a violation itself becomes permissible and is soon viewed as a law in its own right.

What should the victims do? What redress could their families have? How might they complain?

Absurd! The outcome was predictable all along, the circumstances (even when surprising or shocking) always in essence expected and unexceptional. Hardly worth investigating, one might say. But to the great detective it was an ever-present rebuke, his one failing. It was his only shame, the dawning of his declination, the bitterness in his memoirs, the silence of his final retirement. There were powers he did not have, powers possessed by none but the gods.

The Dam

Once the dams were finished, the Yangtze heaved its shoulders as if it could elbow its way out of the gorges. Scattered tribes of monkeys shrieked up the hillside as the level rose and groves of orange trees sank beneath the water.

Were there no warnings?

'Oh, yes. We had time to relocate our ancestors.'

Were there no protests?

'Oh, yes. There were many farmers imprisoned.'

Was there no time to become accustomed to the loss of the land?

'After the first dam, the river was sixty feet higher. We moved the notices of objection further up the mountain.'

Have you now accepted the need for this work? Do you acknowledge the miraculous power of the contained water?

'It takes three hours to rise through the five locks, each lock gate weighing 800 tons. There was a problem, but the villagers have understood that it is for the greater good, and now they flock to the electrified cities.'

But there are still coffins in the high fissures in the cliff face, large black butterflies and clouds of swallows. In the inner streams, sturgeon and salamander. The holy pagoda at Shi Baozhai has just escaped the new water level. It has become an island and therefore more mysterious, in the midst of a river like chocolate. You may ascend the steps to the temple and its unchangeable jade smile. What serenity in the Buddha, compared with the tortured Christian grimace!

Perhaps this serenity spreads like water, inching little by little through the dykes of greed, seeping into the querulous lives of thwarted ambition and frustrated satisfactions. The lives of the workers are in any case accustomed to floods. When the Han was over three feet higher than the street-level in Wuhan, the children caught fish under their beds.

A Brief History of the Piano

80 Très-Sec

The humour is a little tart, as if to say: 'This is what the fingers can do, so let them do it. But you and I know very well that it is not quite enough.' There: at a touch they are off again! The sky is Josiah-blue, and the tutor's wig has been laid aside for perspiration.

78 Beau-Fixe

How simple is melody, a natural continuity and variety: the seed, the shoot, the leaf, the flower, the seed! The family assembles. Let us then have refrains, rondos, parterres, but nothing to disturb the tranquillity of the afternoon.

76 Variable

In the furniture of our sensibility the green has modulated into gold, as the bee chooses nectar for the hive and the orchard trees are cut into fretted sounding-boards. In a drawing-room you may now hear whispers and the thudding of the heart at the same time, as the hands continue to move.

74 Vent ou Pluie

Why is it that the rose-and-ochre west brings a tear to the eye? The boy with his hand on the latch of the garden gate is more likely to be leaving than arriving, and of any two notes the second will fall away. Whatever may be carried across an evening lawn is the better for being only half-heard or left untested. Where is everybody?

All is lost! In a fury of isolation the hero's hands descend at the same time from shoulder-height as if to shut the fiend at last in his thundering coffin. A crimson curtain rises to show him doing it again and again. All is not lost!

Rubato

You have the idea of it in your head, of course. You probably wake up from dreams of it, in undeliberated ease, each moment yielding to the next, each movement naturally succeeding the last. But without practice nothing can be achieved. You are left with an innate clumsiness, the stopgap of the extemporised.

Let's start from the beginning. Don't feel humiliated. Don't think I'm putting you down.

It has to be felt here, at the core. Yes? It moves upwards and outwards, to the shoulders and the neck. And it is felt inwards and downwards, even to the backs of the knees, and the shiver in the toes.

Try it. Take it slowly. Move each finger independently. Feel the pressure and the response. Yes? The power doesn't come from the arm. It comes from the wrist and the shoulder. And control of the breathing. Breathe slowly. Concentrate on the stroke and the release. The reach will come from practice. And the tempo.

Now try it this way. Why not use the thumb here? With the fingers climbing a ladder. Yes? Most people of your build would never think of trying this. It needs more of you. Much more.

Does this work for you? Don't strain. Relax. Don't forget to breathe. Again. Do you see? The tempo is everything. Take your time. It is neither slow nor fast, but always a little later than expected. The conclusion will always seem to be postponed. Yes?

How does it feel for you? Is it working? Can you give it more wrist?

Practice makes perfect.

The Sculptor

Musée Rodin

1

The shoreline's million shapes are his greatest rival's studio, but none of these extraordinary works is finished.

2

The smallest sculpture is a law of physics; the largest is nothing less than the universe itself.

3

The weakness of the mountain: the unconnected surface. The strength of the pebble: shoulders flexing against the sac.

4

When the stones were first replanted, they turned into warriors.

5

The jade silkworm spins a garment for the soul.

6

Simplicity is at the service of magic.

7

Stillness is an illusion: even a limbless torso can be seen to be marching.

8

The bronze horseman rides into the public square. Far from being perfect, the sphere is now another form of chaos.

9

The eyes are blind, the sex broken, but the body lives as it has never lived, in the eternity of its shape.

10

For abject worship, a niche; for sceptical appraisal, a pedestal; for oblivion, a museum postcard.

11

The body is restless, searching for the perfect posture that always eludes it.

12

The swell of the buttock blinds us to the shame of the anus.

13

Admiring the spine, we forget the amusement in the face.

14

The fragility of the ankle, the arrogance of the wrist, the invitation of the hip.

15

The neck is the articulated engine of our curiosity.

16

When the knees tauten, we are closest to the earth.

17

In the one place where the significant darkness cannot be created by shape and shadow, the pupils of the eyes are excavated.

18

He never walks behind his sculptures. For him, the distinction between front and back cannot exist, yet he despairs because he cannot gaze in two directions at once.

19

The strength of the hammer; the lightness of the chisel.

20

The block is a cage to be opened and the form to be released. The marble flies like feathers.

21

The chiselling is a devouring. The remains are flecked in his beard.

22

Marble is in love with skin, as skin is in love with light.

23

The surface of the painter is a culpable deceit.

24

To exchange colour for touch and the infinite change of shadow. And then to reclaim colour.

25

The birth of Venus, the adoration of Psyche, the punishment of Francesca: myth is a licence to examine the extended female form.

26

The mouths of the Sirens are open in eternal song that only he can hear.

27

Juliet embraces the rock that Romeo is escaping from; their swoon is a yielding to its weight.

28

The women are doomed not for their love for each other, but because they are looking at us: the one is excited by the other's knee, whose own haunches are, however, offered to us.

29

His figures always crouch, whether in shrunken terror or in furtive delight; this is because he works from square blocks of marble.

30

From the front, spread legs, a shameless curiosity; from the back, hunched shoulders, a penitential vulnerability.

31

The mind's ostentations (hats, furs, jokes) are beyond his skill to represent. This disturbs the visitors to his studio.

32

The face is a mask at an angle of ecstasy or self-admiration.

33

The infinite drama of space: what was confined is liberated; the finite drama of time: the nose of Icarus a split second before the marble splashes.

34

Everything that is given is finally to be taken away, firstly movement, lastly light.

35

In the winter garden, the snow on shoulders is heavier than their bronze.

Flower, Quartet, Mask

To dignify a room needs no more than unusual attention to the usual. The corner of a glass table with the CD case lying on it, the orchid above still flowering after six months. It's as though a challenge has been issued to time itself. The bronze face of a girl in sleep or ecstasy makes no comment upon the competing efforts of these things to behave as if they could control time. The orchid's petals, like pink propellers frozen in a downwards plunge, a suspended cataclysm, have dared to endure; the music, whose case it is, has moved away on its own, as if to expend itself. One is still, one enlarged. Yet only one is growing unpredictably; the other knows its direction and directions. Does it matter? Both are doomed. Each outwits regulation for the time it takes, and for what time takes from it. The laser will eventually have nothing left spinning to decode, and the stalk will cease to transmit the life that qualifies stillness in the veined blush of the flower. Only the bronze face is content to be measured by time. Her eyes are narrowed, and her slight smile suspends all clocks. Sharing this for the moment that I drain my glass, I reflect that the page is no partisan. Everything has some claim upon it equally. They were all set upon their courses, and must see them through. The page woos them, but they make no response other than to be themselves. Eventually the page apologises, and is silent.

The Names of Fields

When we first stumbled back into those uplands, the farmsteads
of our ancestors had already collapsed. Thistles stood sentry
over grassed boulders. Thorn crowded cracked hearths. But
was our dawn resolve any stronger? Hardly. Not far from *cae
rwyn*, field of the ruin, lies the *pant y diogi*, hollow of laziness,
with not a stone lifted unless it were further to reduce the
shallow turfed remains. Or perhaps to divide the portioned
fields among the hopeful kin, walls radiating from that
remembered patriarchal centre.

But no one can be idle for long, and the land must be
prepared for an age of maps and saints. To name the fields
as cows are named is to expect something of them, or to
yield a point, like *llain randres*, strips to be shared with
cousins from a distant valley, or *cae cyd*, held in common
with Cwm, but nonetheless jealously guarded. Oh, we know
our territory! Like the bird on the wall, with its bright
scouring eye and its dipping tail.

From *hen gae ucha*, the old upper field, we see the whole
extent of the demesne, as a sheep sees it, should it bother to
look. The eye runs from the stone that no force of men could
move, down to the *hendre*, which of course is entirely made
of moved stones. And just by the house is the best field of all,
stubbled with leeks, where a figure in black comes walking, *cae
llidiard offeiriad*, field of the priest's hurdle, to take his tithe.

What will our children do? If they forget the names of the
fields, they may escape both their uses and curses. And though
even new buildings may fall into disrepair, who knows what
strange plantations and machines will take their place?

Last Words

'Come closer, come closer!'

I was encouraged to approach the bed as a favourite, perhaps as the most reliable recipient of the Bishop's dying wisdom, someone who would not only understand it perfectly, but who could remain detached enough to note it down. In the darkness I could see the corner of the great carved bed head, its arched and tumbling torsos faintly lit by the one bedside candle. The Bishop's hand lay palm upwards, and one finger lifted wearily from the counterpane, though the hand itself remained inert. The tiny inviting gesture of the finger was like nothing so much as the tugging at an invisible kite. It was as though he wanted to keep aloft between us a medium of communication, to keep the air clear, as it were, for the words to be spoken.

The women occupied themselves silently in the shadows, seated with sewing. There was no longer any need for their attendance, for the Bishop had been made as comfortable as possible. If he had had the strength or interest he might have dismissed them, but his attention was on me.

Why do we so often rebel against tributes to our unique qualities? In private, we feel decidedly privileged, ready for our promotion into knowledge and power. But when it comes, an obscure feeling of wilful hostility and resentment falls on us. We are churlish, and we rebel. Should recognition not have come much sooner? And from those with purer motives?

I sat by the bed at a distance deliberately chosen as insultingly deferent, and I leaned towards him inadequately, merely inclining an ear with the minimum of politeness as if to overhear pleasantries, and not, as was clearly his intention, to record a momentous truth.

The Bishop's eyes searched for mine, in an alarmed reproof of my diffidence, and with a great physical effort he reached over and grasped my fingers. With a frown, he shook my fingers to and fro. It felt, feeble as it was, the ghost of a reproof. I was doing myself a disservice by my aloofness. After all, the Bishop had now no wish to control me. He was dying, and this was a private struggle to achieve, at the other end of life from the struggle to be born, his own sense of authenticity of being.

But I thought him a mere baby, as selfish still in his quest as a baby would be, howling for some physical relief from discomfort. This pose of sublime knowledge, the awfulness of finality, the ceremony of annunciation, constituted nothing more than a ruse to prop up his self-esteem. Why should he have any concern for me at all?

His lips worked silently in the gloom, struggling against dryness to form words. Even the women put down their sewing, in respect for this heroic moment when, as they had come to believe, the Bishop would mark his deliverance with a statement that would provide an answer to their life-long questioning service. Somewhere a clock ticked like dripping water.

And I could not prevent my resentful rage from breaking out into a great shout of truculent laughter.

Cross-bones

Grown older, and feeling the first signs of muscular fatigue, I have come to think more and more about the long traditions of the box. It isn't that I fear failure, or want to change anything. Really, I am quite happy with the box, and no amount of temporary stiffness (alarming as it sometimes is) would persuade me into making it slightly larger. But as these thoughts occur to me, only to be comfortably put to one side, I am left remembering that great decision of my youth, not at the outset to relax the given conditions in the timidity of my inexperience (which would have been perfectly understood, and immediately forgiven) but in fact *to make the box smaller.*

There is no concealing the fact that despite the personal satisfaction of entering the box, such that a performance needs no witness, no wonder, and no applause, it is in reality an intensely competitive business. To inherit the tradition is to accept a challenge that will be fiercely scrutinised by one's peers. One tiny miscalculation and one would never hear the end of it. A failure in performance would have been unthinkable. You will see, then, that at the outset a small adjustment in one's favour would be an understandable preparation for a lifetime of selfless devotion, by no means a subterfuge, hardly a weakness.

But to make the act harder, and from the very beginning! Did this imply an overweening confidence in the years of private preparation? Perhaps it might be taken as a criticism of the tradition I had inherited. It might be acknowledged with a grudging admiration as belonging to the natural effrontery of the young. My predecessors had learned to make a great rigmarole of increased bondage, as though only the tightest of straps could assist something as unwieldy as a naturally muscular human body into the confines of a crimson metal box less than two feet cubed. But I carelessly abandoned the harness altogether, while reducing the size of the box by visible inches.

The daring of it made my heart beat faster. At the first performance I left one arm quite outside the box. It waved cheerfully at the onlookers and pushed my head this way and that way as though it had no idea what to do with it, while the head glared back at the bullying arm in comic resentment. I made it seem that there was no room for my skull in the box, which was demonstrably chock-full of my already carefully folded cross-bones. And even if there had been, how could the arm have possibly followed it?

Well, there was an answer, and it lay in the dislocation of more bones than my nearest rivals had ever thought it possible to dislocate. And this, too, without the secret assistance of the harness. All was done naturally with small, barely noticeable twitches and jerks of the body under the cover of exaggerated stretches and yawns, as though I were simply preparing for a comfortable night's rest. The folding and inserting of the limbs certainly looked perfectly natural, and was accomplished with a fluid movement while talking happy rubbish to the onlookers. I made it seem like the easiest thing in the world.

But what is it about an audience that makes them so fickle? What is it that upsets them? They laughed at my disrobing. They laughed at my skeletal body. They laughed at the to-and-fro between my evasive and reluctant head and the commandeering arm.

Once entirely in the box, however, once my disappearing fingers had finally flipped down the lid, I failed to please them. They looked again at the tiny box left isolated on the stage, and could hardly believe that I was inside. Yes, they had seen me fold myself inside, but now that I was no longer visible it did not seem possible. There must be some trick. But they could not see what the trick was.

It was not even like a suitcase. Women have been dismembered, and their remains left at the Lost Property Offices of railway stations in suitcases. But this was so small! It was little more than a hat box, or the container of a chamber-pot. And when my assistant came to take it away, hoisting it under his arm with an ostentatious little grunt, and pretending to stagger, their confusion was complete.

'We saw him get in,' they said. 'The floor there is solid. There is no trapdoor. And yet . . . and yet he surely cannot be in that tiny box!'

I could hear the general murmur and wonderment, and it had a strange effect on me, as though I had indeed achieved an impossible disappearance. As though one minute I had been myself, erect, articulate, conversational, and then suddenly had been folded away into nothing. As though I were not in the box after all. And because I had no means of revealing myself, and was from then on entirely at the mercy of my assistant, it hardly seemed to matter where I was. He could have walked away with me into another life, or abandoned me, like one of those Lost Property victims.

This successful removal from life is a rare thing. It has been achieved by a few saints and holy men, and perhaps by some others for whom the body has become, when all is said and done, something of an embarrassment.

Acknowledgements

Grateful acknowledgements are made to the editors of the following, in which some of these prose poems first appeared: *Alhambra Poetry Calendar 2007, Earls Court, European English Messenger* (journal of the European Society for the Study of English), *Footfall, Kilometer Zero 03* (Paris), *London Magazine, Magdalen College Record, Oxford Magazine, Poetry Nation Review, Poetry Review, Poetry Wales, Shing Wan* (Hong Kong), *Times Literary Supplement, Vico Acitillo 124.*

'The Orange Lily' and 'The Cricket on the Table' formed, with other poems of mine, part of a musical sequence called 'A Terrace in Corsica', set by Liz Dobson and Mica Levi, commissioned by Rolf Hind for the Society for the Promotion of New Music, and performed at Wilton's Music Hall in 2007.